We Follow the Voice

Amazing
'God-Stories'
from His Children

Volume I

by Selma Sales

Published in Ardmore, Alabama by Selma Sales
followingthevoice@gmail.com

ISBN 978-1-7377105-0-9

Printed in the United States of America.

DEDICATION

We Follow the Voice is dedicated to Community of Hope, an organization committed to building a residential community where the chronically homeless can find a job within their restoration works program and pay for affordable homes while receiving the help they need to regain their lives.

Please keep the COH and similar organizations in your prayers as they work together, bringing the homeless home.

ACKNOWLEDGEMENTS

A book is never the result of just one person. First giving honor to God for providing the book vision. Thanks to my husband Michael, continued love, and support throughout this project.

A special thanks to Mandy Kilgore and the Community of Hope team for faithfully gathering God-stories from people in the community.

Thanks to all the co-authors for sharing stories and testimonies of how the Voice impacted their lives.

My thanks, of course, also goes to Jerry Ross for the outstanding cover design, and Dr. Jerod Patterson for his superb editing.

Also, thanks to Adrianne Hillman for writing such a timely Forward.

FORWARD

If you have picked up this book, you may think that hearing God's voice feels impossible. Between the many loud voices and the relentless assault of media and other messaging, not to mention the booming cacophony of our thoughts swirling around in our heads, it can seem unlikely that you will hear any decipherable messages that the spirit of God is trying to reveal to you. It is difficult in our culture to listen to ACTUAL sounds above the fray, let alone a voice with no sound. The miracle of hearing God's voice is that it is found in the silence. Interestingly, it is also in the mindful silence that we can tap into the true desires of our hearts. When we invite God into our hearts--our one true dwelling place--He miraculously meets us there, and if we are listening, He reveals Himself to us. When we answer the call, He reveals that He can utilize us to carry out His infinitely beautiful work. Our job is to say "YES." I realize that I am making it sound relatively straightforward. While it is simple in practice, hearing the Voice is a complex thing to accomplish. It can be done, though. I am living proof.

I did not believe that "hearing the voice of God" was real before the day that I heard God speak directly to me. His words were, "You are going to serve the homeless." I had never "heard a voice" in any discernible way in my entire life, and it startled me. Had I imagined it? Was it a figment of a daydream? I was sitting in church--on the front row-- listening to an amazing sermon that had opened my heart in a significant way. It was not about service, as I recall. Well, to be completely honest, I do not recall much before that booming voice came through. All I remember is how it felt. My heart was open, and it was fertile ground for this experience.

And my answer to the loud boom?

"Uh, no. I don't think so, God. I have never served in the homeless realm. Too scary. But I will think about it! Thanks, but that is probably a 'no thanks!'"

Well, it was only three weeks before a member of the board of a local non-profit shelter reached out and asked me to fill the vacant board seat of a person who had suddenly passed away.

My thought was, "There it is. God wants me to sit on this board, and He was just preparing me to say yes! This will be fun! And EASY! YAY!"

And God laughed and laughed. (At least that is how I imagine it went for Him.)

I accepted the position. Immediately, I struggled with what I heard at the meetings about our neighbors experiencing homelessness and how the organization was treating them itself. I realized our organization was viewed as a resource for these folks in need. But our attitude towards them was as damaging as the public. How could we ever help them and show them the love and nature of Jesus by treating them as less than beloved? I immediately wanted to quit and kept asking God to release me from this obligation I had created for myself. I was not hopeful that I could produce enough change in the organization's culture to guide it to a place of compassion and dignity for the outcast and marginalized population we served. I could feel my heart hardening.

Then, one afternoon I listened to Jen Hatmaker's For The Love podcast, and she had a special guest. His name was Alan Graham. He was promoting his new book, Welcome Homeless, and Jen proclaimed that anyone working within the homeless community should familiarize themselves with Alan's work. At that time, Alan's non-profit in Austin, Texas, Mobile Loaves & Fishes, had recently built the nation's first master-planned community to lift neighbors experiencing chronic homelessness off the streets. For twenty years before the build, Alan's team had been feeding folks stranded on the streets with an innovative mobile food truck operation.

His work immediately struck me. That very day, I wrote to Alan. I told him I thought our community had a heart problem and asked if he had come speak at a fundraiser to help teach people a unique way to love people. He wrote right back and agreed to come to my hometown, but only if I came to see him and the Community First! Village first. I agreed.

Mobile Loaves & Fishes hosts symposia three times a year to introduce people to their model and mission. After I agreed, I realized that the dates for their upcoming symposium were not going to work for my schedule. Plus, I was not in a big rush. I planned to learn and absorb this model and organizational vision, go back home, and share it with people that could implement it. I did not have intentions of implementing it.

I mean, I had a life, kids, a life coaching career, an upcoming podcast, and plans to author a book! I would just be the messenger of this good news, and someone else could take on the enormous task of creating a master-planned community for the homeless population in our hometown. I would be on the board, go to the groundbreaking, help with fundraisers... be in a supportive role.

And God laughed and laughed.

In a nutshell, my podcast/career/book was derailed when my youngest son broke his femur, caught MRSA staph from the pins used to keep the shattered bone in place, and was placed in a body cast. I became his nursemaid and put everything on hold for six months. Just when he was healing, a symposium date came up, and I was able to go with a newly cleared schedule. I felt a divine tingle when I realized that God had carefully woven all of this. Even my son's pain was not in vain.

When I got to Community First! Village, I felt as if I had

walked into the closest thing to heaven on earth there could be. The love and peace that I felt walking around that place changed everything for me. I asked Alan if I could just move out to Austin and get a job onsite at their village. He smiled and replied, "Go back home and create your own. Your community needs you to do this."

I went home. I cried and toiled and begged God to place this call on someone else. I knew what taking this on would mean. It would be a complete life change. I would have to give all of myself to this project to see it become a reality. There was no way I could do this on my own. His answer was, "You won't do this alone. I promise. And you can still write and teach and share the love of Jesus. It can be both."

So, I said yes. And I have had to say yes repeatedly every time I want to quit. I launched Salt + Light Works in early 2019. In the early months of 2022, we will be breaking ground on a 52-unit, master-planned community for people experiencing homelessness in California, the first of its kind in the state. Our food and palliative relief truck also feed 600+ meals a week to people still stranded on the streets.

My heart has been softened and changed so many separate times, and in so many ways, I have stopped keeping track since that day I took the call. My only regret is that I fought it so hard and for so long. Through my reluctant acceptance of that call, I gained a better ability to see people clearly and in the ways that God sees them and me. That heart enfleshment has possibly been the greatest gift of listening. What has been incredible is how, all these years of my searching, hoping, hustling, begging, and trying to find meaning and worth in my life, God had so much more in store for me than I could have ever conjured up on my own. I look back and realize how He handed me a call that, over time and an ever-increasing faith in Him, led me back to the most authentic version of myself.

God is in this, and He had a plan. As hard as it has been, I am so glad I listened to The Voice. My hope for you is that you will be able to hear it as well.

– Adrianne Hillman

INTRODUCTION

When talking with people about how the Voice has spoken to me, some commented, "I have heard the Voice too." It was then the Voice said, "Selma, ask people to write short stories of their encounter with the Voice and publish them in your next book." Yes, I heeded His guidance.

Inspired by the many stories submitted, I was impressed to title this book:

We Follow the Voice
Amazing *"God-stories"* From His Children

This book is about the Voice speaking to people in present times and shares its impact on their lives. I pray that readers will listen for God's voice and form an eternal relationship with Him.

The Bible records God communicating with people in days of old:

- **Moses** – So Moses thought, "I will go over and see this strange sight—why the bush does not burn up." When the Lord saw that he had gone over to look, God called to him from within the bush, "Moses! Moses!" And Moses said, "Here I am." Exodus 3: 3,4

- **Sarah** - Then one of them said, "I will surely return to you about this time next year, and Sarah your wife will have a son." Now Sarah was listening at the entrance to the tent, which was behind him. Abraham and Sarah were already very old, and Sarah was past the age of childbearing. So, Sarah laughed to herself as she thought, "After I am worn out and my lord is old, will I now have this pleasure?" Genesis 18: 10-15

- **Mary** - In the sixth month of Elizabeth's pregnancy, God sent the angel Gabriel to Nazareth, a town in Galilee, to a virgin pledged to be married to a man named Joseph, a descendant of David. The virgin's name was Mary. The angel went to her and said, "Greetings, you who are highly favored! The Lord is with you." Mary was greatly troubled at his words and wondered what kind of greeting this might be. But the angel said to her, "Do not be afraid, Mary; you have found favor with God. You will conceive and give birth to a son, and you are to call him Jesus. Luke 1: 26-31

- **Saul** - As he neared Damascus on his journey, suddenly a light from heaven flashed around him. He fell to the ground and heard a voice say to him, "Saul, Saul, why do you persecute me?" "Who are you, Lord?" Saul asked. "I am Jesus, whom you are persecuting," he replied. "Now get up and go into the city, and you will be told what you must do." Acts 9: 3-6

God is still speaking. Are you listening? Do you hear?

Selma Sales

We Follow the Voice

Amazing
'God-Stories'
from His Children

Volume I

Publish Another Book?

The Saturday after Thanksgiving 2017, a sharp pain shot through my stomach. My husband drove me to the hospital, and I was diagnosed with pancreatitis. Upon further examination, the doctor discovered a small benign cyst on the outside of my pancreas. A second opinion confirmed the original diagnosis.

Some of my attending doctors recommended Whipple surgery, a complex operation to remove the head of the pancreas, the first part of the small intestine, the gallbladder, and the bile duct. The following night, while fast asleep, I heard the Voice (one I have followed all my life) gently say, "Selma, don't have the surgery." Reluctantly, I accepted this advice. Subsequently, in consultation with my PC doctor, we decided to monitor my pancreas every six months and note any significant changes.

Later, the Voice said to me, "Selma, you have been writing stories about your life and family since you were very young. Now it's time to put them in a book." Thus began my two-year journey, ending with my first published book in December 2019. Following the Voice – From a Shoebox Grave to Eternity was a moving account of my passionate journey through life, guided, protected, and saved by the voice of God.

Since publishing FTV, many readers have told me the Voice has spoken to them, and some have shared their stories. Driving to the Mall recently, my husband and I encountered several homeless people sitting on the sidewalk, asking for help. This troubled me. That night I prayed, asking God to show me how I could help the homeless in our community. While sleeping, the Voice said to me, "Gather stories from people who have heard the Voice speak to them, put them in a book, and use the proceeds from book sales to help the homeless."

Thus, the inspiration for my second book, "We Follow the Voice," inspirational stories of people, primarily Huntsvillians, who have heard the Voice are following His direction and are doing positive work in their communities emerged.

As my husband and I started planning for WFTV, the Voice directed me to align with someone who shared our concern for the homeless. While diligent searching, the Voice led us to Community of Hope, a local organization that shares a compassionate calling to help the homeless in Huntsville secure safe, affordable housing. Additionally, COH believes that in collaboration, there is Synergy (the ability of two or more entities to generate greater value working together than they could be working apart).

In May 2021, I partnered with COH to publish We Follow the Voice, and the proceeds from book sales will assist them in building a residential community to address chronic homelessness in Huntsville, Alabama.

Just weeks after this partnership agreement, I found myself in the hospital, twice with pancreatitis attacks. This time doctors discovered gallstones in my gallbladder and suggested a possible cause for the pancreatitis attacks. They quickly scheduled surgery and removed my gallbladder.

In recovery, I cried out, "Lord, if you want me to help the homeless, why are you letting so much sickness in my life?" The Voice answered, "Selma, I never said your life would be pain and sorrow free, but I promised to be with you through it all."

Now, reflecting on life's journey, I am reminded of Isaiah 40:31, "But they that wait upon the Lord shall renew their strength; they shall mount up with wings as eagles; they shall run, and not be weary; and they shall walk, and not faint." In this promise, I go forward!

Selma Sales

God has been Preparing My Heart for His Calling

Almost four years ago, my phone rang. The number was unknown to me, so I hesitated. It rang again and again. It was a local Huntsville number, so I decided to answer. That action others are tiny yes' to my overwhelming series of yes' that have locked in my commitment to God our Father. John 10:27 reminds us that "My sheep listen to my voice; I know them, and they follow me."

In that phone call, I was introduced to a social worker from Huntsville Hospital. She explained that she was working with a homeless man who could not be released because he was on continuous oxygen. I learned that it is a liability for the hospital to release someone homeless with an oxygen tank back on the streets.

She went on to explain that he did have income because he was a Veteran. I have been working the streets for many years here in Huntsville in serving the homeless. Through that service, I have learned of many resources for our homeless friends. I also would consider myself very resourceful, determined, and compassionate. Regardless of all things mentioned, I was unable to find this Veteran a home. After another six weeks or so in the hospital, we finally received another phone call from a group in Huntsville that was purchasing foreclosed homes and taking a chance on friends that needed a place to stay. We obtained the 75-page lease and worked with a notary. Shortly after, we moved Rickey in.

This home was not anything you would want to say "Yes" to. It was the dirtiest home we had ever been in. When you opened the drawers in the kitchen, roaches ran out. There were holes in the walls and floors. The bathrooms were completely unmentionable. The previous tenants had locked dogs in one of the bedrooms, and the muck and smell were unbearable. Regardless, we had a team come in and clean that home to the best of its ability. We furnished the home with everything needed as Rickey only had the clothes on his back and a backpack. We were blessed to move in with two other veterans as the rent was $650 a month in a terrible neighborhood riddled with gun violence, prostitution, and drugs. We were not ok with this situation but had no other options here in our gorgeous city of Huntsville.

A few weeks went by, and our frustrations continued with this home. We found ourselves in a slum lord situation. The AC unit in the house went out, and it was weeks before the landlord fixed it. The rent continued to rise, as well as the maintenance issues. We were thankful that our friends were housed but frustrated with the constant neglect and the horrifying environment they were exposed to.

I can remember the day that the Holy Spirit came over me. I was in my office, scrolling through social media when I came across a video. I watched an older woman named Emily saying, "I was really just so grateful to get off the streets. I didn't know how much longer I was going to make it." The video shared information about a non-profit organization where the homeless could find a home, jobs, a purpose, and relationships to integrate them back into society. This place connected human to human, heart to heart. "This place is the closest place to heaven on earth." The video ended, and at that moment, this wave crashed over me. This was it. This was the solution for our homeless friends. This video had captured my heart and lit an inextinguishable fire. Isaiah 30:21 says, "Whether you turn to the right or to the left, your ears will hear a voice behind you, saying, 'This is the way, walk in.'"

From that day, almost four years ago till today, I have followed His way. I have listened to Him; He has guided me on this path of providing homes to the homeless. I have walked into this solution-based approach for being the salt of the earth and serving Him to the best of my ability. I am committed to God on a level that is hard to explain. Through Him, we will provide homes and so much more for our homeless brothers and sisters within Community of Hope, restoring hope to the hopeless through Him, one friend at a time.

Mandy Kilgore
Huntsville Community of Hope
Founder, President, and Chief Goodness Officer
Huntsville, AL

The Voice Teaches

God's voice taught me the importance of loving my neighbor, and He went further and told me who my neighbor is. It is not just that man and woman who lives next door to me or across the street. It is not just the person who lives across town or the country. His voice told me that everybody on this planet is my neighbor, and we are all walking a path heading straight into eternity. He told me my responsibility in love is to show my neighbors how to Love and help carry anyone struggling as they walk their path.

That has led me to the awesome gift of being able to lend a shoulder for someone to cry on, an arm and hand to help pick up or carry someone another step, another day, another week!

The joy that floods my soul from this gift that I received from His lovely voice is beyond measure, and my eternal gratitude is directed to Him, the author of Love!
John 3.16

Tom Milner

The Journey

When we finally moved into our home in West Virginia, it was delightful. Our friends laughed and made every West Virginian joke ever made, but we did not let that trouble us a bit. After all, we have always lived with the philosophy "THINK DIFFERENT." The only thing that had given us pause was when more people decided to take the leap and move here too. That is when a 1.2-hour drive turned into two, then three, and sometimes four-hour drive one way. We adjusted, though, and looked at it as we were in our peace when we got home.

One day in the winter of 2010, February to be exact, we had the biggest snowstorm that had ever hit Washington, DC, Maryland, Virginia, and West Virginia. They called it 'Snowmaggdon.' The Federal government released all federal employees at around noon that day, anticipating the severe storm that was coming to enable employees to try and get home safely. Cheryl and I had no less than a two-hour drive ahead of us and probably longer with the snow already starting. We were driving Cheryl's Dodge Ram, feeling secure that we were at least in a larger vehicle on the road. Unfortunately, we were not weighted down in the pick-up bed, which was not good on some untreated highways between Washington and West Virginia. Maryland, fortunately, had pre-treated their roads with a good coat of brine.

By the time we reached the northwestern part of Maryland, the snow had begun to come down heavy. When we got to the border of Maryland and West Virginia and crossed over into West Virginia, we immediately could feel that DOT had not treated the roads at all. The type of snow that had dusted the I81 corridor was like an ice-skating rink for the Dodge. I do not know your familiarity with the I81 corridor; it is a major tractor-trailer trucking route for transporting goods from the east to the south and west. It is considered a very treacherous thoroughfare when driving because of the major accidents on this stretch of Interstate. We crossed over into West Virginia and cautiously traveled approximately a mile when the rear end of the pick-up fishtailed and began to spin out of control on the highway. It turned from the far-right lane to the center median and landed parallel to the center median guardrail facing the oncoming traffic. We shouted our prayers to the Father to please protect us and keep the three tractor-trailers that were bearing down behind us from losing control and hitting us. The Holy Spirit took control of the vehicle and placed it perfectly out of traffic and safely in the median without hitting the guard rail or anything else. We were badly shaken but okay. We could see our way clear to ease back onto the highway and turn around in the right direction to continue our journey home. That storm locked us and this part of the country down for two weeks.

We were blessed and protected with His grace, just as we ask Him to do every morning before we leave our home to begin the long road trip to and from work. Thank you, Jesus; thank you, Lord.

Cheryl Youngblood Sales and Linda Youngblood Sales

Teach What Grade?

Since I was four years old, I knew that I wanted to teach children. I wanted to make a positive impact on young lives and help them yearn to learn. Because I knew my calling in life, it made my educational pathway easy to chart; however, I met a fork in the road after completing my master's degree program. What grade should I teach- lower elementary (K-3) or upper elementary (4-6)?

I was certified to teach any grade between kindergarten and sixth. Still, after my student teaching experience, I knew that I wanted to teach upper elementary beyond a shadow of a doubt. I loved the fact that the scholars in upper elementary already knew how to read, and they could work on projects independently. I could hold a conversation with these older scholars. However, out of the job offers I had in front of me, all of them were for teaching Kindergarten or first grade. As I prayed about what to do, the Lord asked me one important question, "Which grade levels do you have the most experience teaching?" As I reflected on that question, I realized that most of my experience was with lower elementary students. I continued to complain and groan to God as the summer progressed. I told the Lord, "I don't want to teach young children. They pick their nose, and they don't cover their mouth when they cough and sneeze." God did not reply. Finally, a position opened for me to teach fourth grade, and I hopped on it.

I was so excited as I entered my first year of teaching. I had the perfect class size, and I was living in a brand-new city. As the first few weeks passed, I started to see that I should have done it God's way. As the challenges began to mount in my "perfect classroom" and my patience grew thinner and thinner with a couple of the scholars, I saw that I was about to learn a valuable lesson. Then I started having challenges from parents, and my first year began to spiral out of control. I sought assistance from several classmates and mentor teachers, but it was only a band-aid for the numerous challenges I faced every week. First-year teachers generally have a rough year, but in my heart, I knew that the reason for these trials was because I went against God's grade-level career path.

As I prepared to finish my first year of teaching, I was drained emotionally, mentally, and physically. Although I loved getting up each morning and working with my scholars, the support system I thought I had at the school crumbled. I had several prayer sessions with God, pleading for deliverance from this situation. God kept it simple. He asked me, "Are you ready to do it My way?" Without hesitation, I said, "Yes, please Lord, yes!" I quickly applied for a new teaching position at other schools in the area. When the administration would ask me about my grade level interest, I would promptly reply, "Lower elementary," with a smile. The Lord opened an incredibly special door, and I have been working with scholars in Pre-K 4 and Kindergarten for over ten years. I love my scholars and my new support system so much and look forward to following God's way each day.

"Your ears will hear a word behind you, 'This is the way, walk in it,' whenever you turn to the right or to the left." Isaiah 30:21. I heard the Voice and chose to go my own way, but the Lord was patient with me and waited for me to come back to the path He had for me.

Chanel Nance
Chanel A. (Sales) Nance is the author of Shower Talk, a book of inspirational poetry and devotional thoughts. An early childhood educator by day and a writer on weekends. She enjoys working with children, writing, reading, sleeping, eating and most importantly, spending time in prayer.

Medicine - The Good – The Bad

A few years ago, I found myself locked inside of my body. I did not realize it at the time, but my family did. I began to act strange to them. I was short-tempered, had trouble remembering, and took on a whole other personality. My daughter and husband thought I was developing early stages of Alzheimer's. This went on for a little over a year. During that time, I had even started a new job, and I remember thinking that the things I was to be learning should not be that difficult. Even though I felt like something was not right, I thought it was everyone else.

Then one night, I was in a deep sleep when I suddenly woke up hearing the subtle and gentle voice of my Lord. All He said was for me to stop taking that medicine. I know it was Him because I did not even question it.

The next day, I called my doctor and asked him to wean myself off the medicine. I do not remember much about that year.

It is like I lost time, but I do know God came to my rescue, as always, and put my life back together. I am so grateful for His mercy and grace.

C. Bryant

Hearing and Obeying God's Voice

One morning around 7am in 1997, I prepared myself for work when the Lord spoke to me. I had a sister-in-law who had been diagnosed years earlier with Lupus. The Lord spoke into my spirit to call her. My response was, "I will call her when I come home from work." Again, the Holy Spirit said to me, "you need to call her now;" my response was, "I will call her when I come home from work."

I was in a training class on a fixed shift, and I would be late getting to work if I made the call at that time. Again, the Holy Spirit spoke to me about calling my sister-in-law. This time I was told of the guilt, I would feel if something happened to her, and I did not call when I had the opportunity. This time my response was, "Ok, ok. I will just be late for work."

I made the call, and I am so glad I did. My sister-in-law was mentally and emotionally in a bad place. When I called, she shared that her siblings who lived within walking distance did not call or come by to check on her knowing she was ill. The Lord spoke to my spirit, and I began sharing His words with her. The Lord told me to tell her that it did not matter if her family called her or stopped over to see her.

He used me to be His spokesperson to let her know that

He was checking on her and that He loves her and would never leave her.

My sister-in-law and I had numerous conversations after that but none so intense and meaningful.

One months later, she was found dead in her bathtub. The cause of death was accidental drowning.

I am so grateful the Lord used me as His messenger.

Mildred Clemons

Papa Euley

I have heard God's voice so many times, but the one I choose to share involves my love for my Papa, who passed away in 1995 from cancer. He was the first person I had to "watch" suffer and die, unable to help. He was my world. He played with me outside, taught me to ride a bike, taught me how to drive, and did so many other things. He kept our yards mowed, and the smell of freshly cut grass always brought a smile. I grew up playing the piano at church, and he would help with the singing. He could play the fiddle better than anybody, and I would play along with him on the piano. I pass by the place he always worked and can envision him squatted down in the doorway having a smoke break and speaking to people passing by. He also loved to sit on his porch and listen to the radio each day. He loved a cold glass of milk and would turn his glass upside down on his plate when finished with it. I have so many wonderful memories of him. Sometimes in my quiet time, I can still hear him whistling in the wind and occasionally catch a whiff of his Winston cigarettes.

Papa died the year after I married and did not get to meet any of his great-grandchildren. Being such a close family, we had grown up with our cousins and spent a great deal of time with him and our Mama. With the birth of my first child, I began missing him even more and was so sad that I had not gotten to share this joyous occasion with him. My children are my whole world, and I knew he would have been so proud of my daughter Katie.

One night after several weeks of wishing he could have met her; I had the most vivid dream I have ever had. I do not doubt that it was God's way of comforting me. Papa came to me in my dream, wearing his black jeans, blue shirt, and black shoes that he wore quite often. We did not say a word in my dream. He simply reached for my hand and led me into Katie's room, where she was asleep in her crib. He looked at Katie, then at me, and smiled his half-grin. He was gone as quickly as he had appeared.

From that moment, I never thought of Papa with sadness because he had never seen Katie but with peace that he knew her and was watching over her. All of Papa's great-grandchildren have been told about Papa so much that they almost "know" him. We only recently lost our Mama, and she had filled them and all of us with stories about Papa. We miss them both so much. It is no longer with sadness, though.

I am so thankful for the relationship I had with my Papa and for the closeness of our family. While I think of him and Mama daily, I have the assurance of where they are and that we will see them both again.

Jenny Wynn

The Roland Gresham Story

I was born in 1956 in Nashville, Tennessee. My father was a Jazz Guitarist, and jazz music was what I heard from the day I was born because my dad practiced his jazz music every day. When I was six years old, my father showed me how to play three chords on the guitar: C, G, & F. I continued to practice playing my guitar every day, and by the age of fifteen, I could play along with anything that I heard on the radio.

When I was fourteen, I was invited to be the guitarist for a four-piece band. I joined them for several gigs over three months. It was not long before I realized that that the nightclub atmosphere was not right for me. Just about everyone there was drinking and smoking, something I had not seen at home. My parents did not smoke or drink. I decided to sever my relationship with that band. I became a Christian at age 16 and began playing selections during the church services, which led to requests for me to play at weddings and banquets.

In the late 1970s, I began a career in construction, working as an Electrician. Some of the guys would bring out a guitar and ask me to play for them during some of our lunch breaks. Several of my coworkers suggested that I make a living playing my guitar and not doing construction work. Even though it sounded like a good idea, I was not convinced that I could succeed playing my guitar for a living. One day in April 1988, while I was relaxing at home in deep thought, a voice spoke softly, "Ronald, use your talent for me." The next day, I decided to leave the construction trade and dedicate my musical talent to full-time ministry.

I began playing at churches in Nashville, Tennessee, and the surrounding states, receiving love offerings, and making my recordings available. It was not hard to see that God was blessing my efforts. Someone suggested that I play at a large Baptist church in California during one of my visits there. So, I decided to take five hundred cassette tapes with me. I shared one selection during the Sunday morning service and sold three hundred cassette tapes after the service. It was then I knew that I had made the right decision. Since that time, I have played at churches throughout the United States. The Lord has blessed me to play internationally in London, England, Toronto, Canada, Bermuda, Jamaica, and the US Virgin Islands. I have also performed on several television programs. I have even shared the stage with notable artists such as Richard Smallwood, Take Six, Helen Baylor, Vickie Winans, and many others.

As I look back over the years, I can tell that God has had His hand on my musical path. Even though there were times when it appeared that things were not working out, I continued to trust God. So far, He has never let me down. Always trust in the Lord!

Roland Gresham

When God says Move – Move!

When Jesus tells us in Matthew 17:20 to "have faith as small as a mustard seed...nothing will be impossible," He means it literally. Here is one of my stories.

It was 2008, and the housing market was in tatters. I was an insurance agent with a big insurance company, but honestly, I was really struggling. One day at work, as I read my Bible, I was in the book of Deuteronomy, and I read an obscure passage that got stuck in my head. It said, "Ye have compassed this mountain long enough: turn you northward" (Deuteronomy 2:3 KJV). This passage stuck with me. Several weeks later, I was in my car on my way to work, praying and asking God if it were Him speaking to me? If it were, give me a sign because this was a big deal, and I would need to resign from my position, which meant talking to the Boss, finding a realtor, finding a new house, and selling my farm, all the excuses of which I could think. God must have laughed.

My boss worked in an office two hours away from me. That morning for only the third time in four years, the boss came into my office. Shortly after talking to my boss and telling him I had to resign (he talked me into applying for a transfer), a new customer who was a realtor came in!

Then I went home and told my wife we were moving. She laughed and said, "Yeah, sure. How are we going to do that?" We have a farm and eight horses." I told her, "I don't know, but God told me to go up North so He will work it out." From that point on, I left everything up to God. I talked to the manager in Huntsville, and he allowed me to transfer to a small regional office in the North. I began looking for a farm. One day I drove down a country road and had an inexplicable urge to stop at a house where some people had gathered in a breezeway. One of the people was a Marine. (I am a Marine.) They did not know of any place for sale, but there was a property owned by a fellow just down the street who had recently retired from the Navy. He had fenced land, a barn, and no animals! I went down the street and talked to him. His name was Steven. He agreed to board my animals for $100 a month to rent a pasture, and oh, by the way, I found out his wife was a realtor.

Events happened, and my wife and I were without a place to stay. Steven and Tracy offered to let us stay with them, which we did for four months. Meanwhile, we looked for a place of our own. We found a place that we had tried to buy three times, but it never went through. Finally, I looked to the sky and said, "I have got it, God. You don't want me to buy this house." A short time later, I lost my job and went from earning a significant amount of money to only $9.00 an hour.

In February of 2009, we rented a home in town and signed a one-year lease. In May, Steven and Tracy asked if we wanted to rent their place, where our horses now were). Because three months remained on our current one-year lease, I thought I could not, but God worked things out, and when we asked the property manager about getting out of the lease, she said the owner had told her to put it up for sale, and if it sold, we could get out of the lease. Less than 30 days later, there was a sales contract on the house, and we could move.

Meanwhile, I had to file bankruptcy because of my low-paying job. Then, I got a job offer working with Veterans. Two years later, I was promoted to Director of the organization. Shortly after my promotion, I received a call asking if we wanted to buy the house. I do not know how it is a God thing, but I could buy my house two years after the bankruptcy.

Bill Koch
Chief Operations Officer
Still Serving Veterans

Blessings from Above

My life has been incredible since birth. I was born into a Christian family where my grandfather was a minister in the Seventh-day Adventist Church and did church planting all along the East Coast.

I was truly fortunate that God led me to a devoted husband, who I met at a Christian university. Being a homemaker, we sacrificed much to send our children to church schools. It has paid off because all our children still have close, personal relationships with the Lord. I praise God every day.

Back in 2004, I was diagnosed with cancer. The doctor called my husband and said my condition was severe, and the prognosis was bleak. We were a praying family, and many of my friends and family were praying for me. God heard our prayers.

Fast forward to 2021. I have been free from cancer for 17+ years. It pays to "Follow the Voice." I am so thankful for God's blessing on my family, and we look forward to meeting the One who made it possible for us to inherit His kingdom.

Beverley Phipps

Attitude of Gratitude

My story begins with being raised in a Christ-loving family, the youngest of six siblings. We went to church every Sunday and participated in all the church activities.

As a teenager, I became pregnant, and though I was offered a contract to have a safe abortion, I refused. The father and I got married, we had three boys, then after ten years, we divorced. Less than a year later, we remarried, that time for five years, and later divorced again. My heart had been broken again.

I moved to Florida with my youngest son Mike, 13. After a while, my middle son, Jim, moved in with me, then later, my oldest Bob. When my baby was sixteen, he went back to visit his dad for a summer. When I went back to celebrate my folks' 50th anniversary and bring Mike home, he said he would stay with his dad, another heartbreak.

With each heartbreak in my life, God was there to pick me up again. I eventually found a husband who I loved and who loved me.

Years later, Mike and his wife joined the Branch Davidians, which was so sad. I asked God why this had to be. I had prayed so hard that when he left his dad and moved to Florida, he would be safe and find a church. But why the Davidians?

Our government attacked the church and killed most of the Davidians. Michael, at age 29, was killed. Thank God I was able to gain protective custody of his three-year-old son. I was more than heartbroken; I was devastated. First, I lost my beloved son. My government killed him; thus, I lost my beloved country after my parents had taught me to be so patriotic. What else did they teach me about God? Losing a son, my country, and God left me an empty shell.

I then went back to church in the hope of finding peace. Frankly, church did not help that much. I finally told God that I was tired and that searching for Him was fruitless. I said, "Lord, if You want me, come and get me."

Very soon after that prayer, I met a woman who then worked with me for ten years, helping me to rebuild my life. I analyzed, prayed, and worked hard at recovery. I learned, of course, that all things happen for a purpose. Those three boys had taught me about unconditional love, compassion, and how not to take things for granted. The first husband, through the two divorces, taught me I am strong and can handle grief and can take care of myself. My Dad and two brothers died, then Mike was killed from this sorrow. I learned that only through forgiveness would I start to heal. Once I decided to forgive, things began to get better.

I have a few mantras that came to mind while healing from all this horrible grief.

The question is not "Why me?" It is "What am I to learn from this?"

This, too, will pass. With God, all things are possible.

Then another brother and my sister died, leaving me with only one surviving sibling. I was able to handle this much better.

However, my middle son, Jim, died from congestive heart failure. He was only at 56. His death was another time of sadness, followed 11 months later by the death of my husband of almost 40 years. At this time, I again appealed to God with "God, I cannot go through this again!" Well, about 20 minutes later, the thought came into my head, "Approach from a different perspective." I think this must have been God answering my inappropriate kind of angry prayer.

I chose the ATTITUDE OF GRATITUDE for the limited time I was allowed to have these beloved people in my life! Best blessing ever! Now, if I start to get down and sad, I tell myself, "Where is that attitude of gratitude?" It works like a charm! Thanks to God!

Latest mantra: Where is that attitude of gratitude!

PS: Thank God I did not have that abortion! I still have that first baby boy in my life.

Sandy Connizzo

First to Orion

I vividly remember the indelible words, "I will save more souls from the success of this movie than I did with the brick-and-mortar building in Cummings Research Park." While I was reviewing the awards from the company my wife and I had founded, I distinctly remember this message that I believe was presented in a Spiritual context. The company was Infinity Technology Inc., an Aerospace-Defense Contracting firm that my wife (Alicia) and I had founded in 1989. The awards were plaques, model aircraft, model spacecraft-Orion, and a flag flown over the U.S. Capitol, at the direction of Senator John Kerry. After 23 years of exceptional success and acute struggles, Alicia and I sold the company in 2011. The movie "First to ORION" (FTO) is about Alicia and Guy Juzang's real-life-gripping inspirational story of faith, hope, and perseverance that inspires all genders and races to dream big and fight for their destinies.

FTO is about two Black computer engineers who start an Aero-Tech Defense firm in Huntsville, Alabama but soon discover that they have the same goals but have opposed methods of reaching them! Their goals are to raise a family and build a prosperous business that creates Hi-Tech jobs, especially for the underutilized. This is a story of the genius of Alicia, who managed the critical balances of work and home. She was a professional woman who took the difficult computer sciences courses and corporate preparatory job to reach this plateau in her career but found herself somewhat resentful that Guy kept pushing her away from the office! Alicia was cautious, detailed, and apathetic about the business objectives to protect the family interests. In contrast, Guy was rash, taking risks to meet the business goals and thinking it would ultimately help the family and employees.

Life-threatening stress, disagreements, and anger arose between them on whether they should have mortgaged their home (while supporting four children) to get the bank's credit line. Bank liquidators and FBI investigators showed up to audit their financials, potentially causing them to lose everything. Their worst fears surfaced when they found out that a high-level employee was trying to sabotage their company by making defamatory comments to their major customer.

Their opposing ideologies and methods came to a boiling point when they were faced with a delayed payroll and how to manage the development deadlines of the operating system of the Air Forces' mission-critical F-22 fighter jet to counter missile attacks from Korea! They persevere, and their faith is rewarded by receiving the following:

- Presidential and Congressional citations and a flag flown over the Capitol in honor of Infinity Technology.

- The development of the F-22 Fighter Jet's Operating System (which took 17 years and 1.5M lines of code) led to being awarded the #1 Small

Business Subcontractor in the U.S. (SBA's National Subcontractor of the year-FY2000).

- Recognized for being the first small business to design, engineer, and fabricate the main engine and other critical parts for the ORION Spacecraft and being named NASA's Dryden's Woman-Owned Business of the Year (2004).

- Either developed or enhanced the operating systems of four major DOD aerospace systems deployed to protect America and allies abroad.

- Developed the operating system architecture for the Army's first digital Apache Helicopter.

- Built the company from 2 to 210 employees and created jobs for many minorities who held prestigious positions with the Government or started their businesses.

After 23 years of phenomenal success, difficult challenges, and perseverance, Guy and Alicia sold their company and turned to focus on what was most important-family. The four children, inspired by their parents' faith, majored in business and the STEM fields.

We often wondered why God allowed so many heavy trials during those 23 years while staggering pockets of success that even the major Aerospace companies envied. However, when I was hanging up those awards, and it became clear that God intended to make a movie out of our experience, it all suddenly made sense!

The movie is in pre-development, and we have attached producers and a director. We are now at the point of hiring the actors, and we have creditable financiers. If you want to follow us, you can view our website (www. FirsttoOrion.com), Instagram First to Orion Movie, or contact Guy Juzang at *guyjuzang@gmail.com.*

| **Guy Juzang**

Everyone Hears a Voice

The voice I hear has been a constant in my life, a means for digesting, understanding, and interacting with my world, and moving forward with courage, even when the future is uncertain. The voice I hear can be harsh or kind, confusing or clarifying. It helps me process ideas and thoughts, so I make primarily good decisions and optimize my life here on earth. It can sometimes deceive me into false, irrational thinking, and it is something every human experiences.

It may surprise you to learn that I do not attribute these inner voices to an external source, unlike many or perhaps all other contributors to this book. For you see (PLEASE DON'T STOP READING), I am an atheist, a humanist, one who has discovered no scientific evidence of a higher being or an external source for those voices. But I experience this inner dialogue just the same and hope my words may be helpful in some way. My perspective just might be one to help you understand your inner voices a bit better, so I hope you will ignore that little voice inside and keep reading.

Consider this. Psychologists have identified inner dialogue that is active every waking moment of our lives. Cultivated in the right, positive way, it can be a powerful tool to help us make good decisions, question what we hear, ponder life and nature, and more. If any of you have been in therapy, you probably have explored that with your therapist. You can learn more about the value of the inner critic and self-talk here: https://ct.counseling.org/2018/12/some-thoughts-on-thoughts-the-inner-critic-and-self-talk/.

Such exploration can even help us process our mistakes and learn from them or alter our behavior. Inner speech shapes how we see the world around us and how we live in it. It plays a role in how we regulate our actions and our thoughts. And regardless of your perspective, the fact is that for every human being, such inner conversations begin as early as age 3, when cognition and language abilities are beginning to develop.

I greatly admire Vygotsky, Piaget, and more recent scientists who can help us understand this human capacity. We are still learning. I encourage you to explore what neuroscientists and other researchers are uncovering about this phenomenon. BUT, as important, now onto the personal, relatable side of this narrative – my voices.

The voices I hear are . . . voices from those who have taught me lessons, those who physically interacted with me, and those whose words inspired and challenged me to think when I read them or heard them, even though we have never personally met. Those are still here physically and those that have died. Humankind continues to progress because we listen to those who have come before. A great aunt of mine once told me, "No one is really gone as long as someone is thinking or talking about them." That is the truth.

The voices are. . . wise sages (we all need a mentor's words to live by) and even those of young children who have not yet been limited by the prejudices of the world and the hatred that is always learned and never innate. Recalling those is keeping a treasure.

The voices are also . . .my intellect, questioning, and higher-level thinking skills of analyzing, synthesizing, and evaluating, hopefully, honed over time and experience. It can encourage, motivate, inspire. The human brain is an amazing organ. This advice from Steve Jobs, founder of Apple Computers, and a brilliant man, is meaningful to me: "Don't let the noise of others' opinions drown out your own inner voice."

No matter what you attribute those inner voices to, evaluate and compare them to the facts we know – that is where those voices can be most helpful and influential in our lives.

I hope you see in this contribution a commonality we can all acknowledge – our humanity allows us to share this cognitive and biological function that represents itself in our inner voices. They can help us become compassionate, thinking, caring, motivated, and inspiring human beings who can make the world a better place, no matter our chosen worldview.

Anonymous

Laundry Room Jesus

I always warned my sweet boys about the truth in "stranger danger." "Do not speak to strangers, stay in our yard, or wander off without asking permission." The boys are now men, and joke that I had not allowed them to play in the yard alone until they were thirteen. That was not entirely true, but almost.

On one of the few occasions that I allowed the boys to

venture outside without me, I was busy in the house getting dinner together and then starting a load of laundry. Suddenly, I could hear an audible voice yelling, "Go check on your boys." I tried to shake it off; after all, we almost lived at a dead end. The only reason you went down our road was to get to one of the houses. There was no through traffic. But in the middle of filling the washer, I dropped everything and ran outside, where my oldest ran to meet me, yelling, "Mama, Caleb is going to that truck in front of our house." I ran around the side into the front yard and saw Caleb steadily walking toward a stranger in an unfamiliar truck. I yelled, and he turned to me, and the truck sped off. Wow.

To this day, I do not know what would have happened had I not heeded that warning and continued doing my chores. There had been an attempted child abduction the same week in Florence, Alabama, and we lived nearby in Killen. It was not the same vehicle, and for some reason, I never believed the two were connected, but I do believe for sure that Jesus was in that laundry room pulling me by the hand to my child.

Sherri Richardson

A Prayed- for- Husband

In 1958, Houston, Texas was a segregated city, yet education in the wards and the ghetto was excellent. As a student of Wheatley High, I often took the city bus to reach home from school. During one of these rides, the thought came to me to pray for my future husband.

St. Elizabeth's Hospital, a Catholic hospital between my home and school, seemed like the ideal place. As a Catholic girl, the quietness and stillness of the chapel seemed to draw me back every day after school, where I prayed for a person I had never met. There were days when I imagined, upon rising from my knees, he would be there behind me, or maybe he would be entering the chapel's swinging doors.

Soon, I was walking down the aisle in my graduation cap and gown, but he had not come yet.

I went to work at Our Mother of Mercy church school, a church and school run by the Jesuit Order. My job was as the secretary to the school's Principal. Several suitors came and went, but none seemed right for me. One of the priests, Father Doyle, even tried to fix me up, but I chickened out at the last minute.

Before I knew it, ten years had passed. I finished business school with an associate degree in business, and Dow Chemical Company hired me as a stenographer, one of the first Black stenographers in Houston. In that position, a young black engineer showed interest in me, but I did not reciprocate his interest.

My next job was thrilling and exciting. For five years, I worked as a flight attendant for Braniff International Airline. Living in and flying out of the Dallas/Fort Worth area was like a dream. Contrary to popular opinion, all flight attendants are not modern Millie's, but some were Christians and members of a Christian flight attendant organization. Various types of guys showed interest, but I was looking for a Christian man, a man like my Baptist father who taught us good Christian values and how to live in this World and remain faithful to God.

One of my roommates at Hostess College introduced me to the Seventh-day Adventist church. It was not what she said but what she did that caught my attention. On Friday evenings before sunset, someone picked her up in a little red sports car and whizzed her off to where I did not know, and every Saturday evening after sunset, she returned. She missed all the parties and dinners with a group of us. When my curiosity got the better of me, I asked her," Gloria, where do you scoot off to every Friday evening?" She then introduced me to the Sabbath. But it was four years later that I came into the church. Shortly after that, I left the Airline, and she pushed me to enroll in Oakwood College. What is Oakwood College? Why would I, a thirty-year-old woman, want to enroll in college? After much prayer, it seemed to me that God wanted it too.

In 1976, I enrolled in Oakwood College, majoring in Religion and planning to become a Bible worker or a missionary. I was sure that God had said no to marriage for me, and I was all right with that. He was my joy, and I needed no one else.

At Freshmen and New Student orientation, a handsome, fine, well-dressed, articulate professional young man was facilitating. He was Director of Counseling at Oakwood and well-educated, with not just one master's degree but two. For some unknown reason he singled me out, asking me, "Do you have any questions?" I sat at the rear of the group and shook my head "No." I watched the girls pushing to be noticed by him, flirting, and asking silly questions. In my mind, he was just another playboy. I dismissed him from my mind.

The following week, I found myself teaching a kindergarten Sabbath school class. Across from my class was another kindergarten class. I looked up, and there he was Lester Morrow, a Kindergarten Sabbath School teacher, seated across from me. When he waved and smiled, I simply ignored him. I rearranged my class setup and turned my back to him and his group. When class was over, I rushed out the door, hoping to escape him, but he caught up with me, introduced himself, and asked my name.

Shortly after that, we began dating. We set boundaries. There would be no petting or anything God would disapprove of, yet I still did not realize this was the man

I had prayed for so long ago.

One night after a date, I entered my room and knelt to pray. Suddenly the room grew very still and quiet. A male voice spoke from behind me, "That's your man!" Turning around, I saw no one. I knew God was telling me that my prayed-for-husband had finally come. I had given up hope after my sister-in-law gave me the name "Antique." And most of my friends had long since married. It seemed to me that I was always the bridesmaid but never the bride.

Years later, I came to realize that God needed to get me to the right place. I was not to marry a Catholic but someone whose beliefs were aligned with the Bible and not with tradition. So, on June 5, 1977, my prayed-for-husband and I were married. We just celebrated our forty-fourth wedding anniversary.

God works in mysterious ways; His wonders to perform!

Ann Morrow

The Relentless Voice

Like a strange song stuck in my head, I kept hearing, "Go check on her. I bet she's cold." Knowing my little girl was old enough to cover herself up, I tried to go back to sleep, but again, I heard, "I bet she's so cold…You're warm under your covers, but she's so cold." The Voice was relentless, so I went to her and found her uncovered. My big fluffy robe she liked to sleep with had slid off into a heap next to her bed, but then I noticed the robe's belt was wrapped around her neck, its weight tightening with gravity's slow pull. Because God still speaks to His people in ways we can hear and understand, I was able to untangle the robe from my daughter's neck. She kept sleeping soundly, safe in the Father's care.

"Listen and hear My Voice; pay attention and hear what I say." Isaiah 28:23

Sally Anne Gist

A Story Bigger than Death

A dimly lit ultrasound room was not the place to mourn. But we knew the sadness was coming. There had been no heartbeat.

Later, I felt nothing. I am supposed to feel anguish. My wife cries. She weeps in gushes that come for seconds at a time, like waves racking her body, like labor contractions. I feel nothing—a void where life used to be.

"Our baby is with Jesus," my wife whispers. "They're still in me – but they're not."

I wrote these words on October 9h, 2019, when our glow of carrying new life was replaced with disorienting grief. Four months later, we experienced our second miscarriage. The tragedy was touching me where I never imagined it could. Through the resulting season of darkness, God tuned our ears to His voice in ways we might not otherwise have heard.

In the months following our first loss, the line "I'm so glad I learned to trust Him" from the hymn Tis So Sweet to Trust in Jesus repeatedly played in my head. That was our reflexive response, clinging to our father with our distress, confusions, and questions. After the second loss, I was angrier. It all felt meaningless. What was the point? Was there a lesson we had not yet learned? Were we presuming upon God that we could or should still get pregnant?

Days after we thought the first miscarriage was over, my wife went into labor and delivered all that was left, and then went into shock, shaking uncontrollably. This was our experience that night in the ER, in her words:

"I was absolutely terrified. I thought I needed the doctor to tell me a couple of specific things to calm down, but I was wrong. I needed Jesus.

Never have I known the sufficiency of God so deep inside of me. The God of the universe met me right there in that room and reassured me He was sufficient."

In the weeks and months following, when we were beset by fear and felt spiritually attacked, we reached out to our community to pray for us. I distinctly remember the vision of our friends as silhouetted warriors, surrounding us, standing between us and the encroaching darkness.

The story of Jesus calming the storm was a recurring encouragement. He did not calm the storm from a safe distance - He did so from within the storm, in the boat with the disciples. We felt that. He is with us in our storms, and that is even better than the absence of them. These were just a few of the many ways we sensed God shepherding us in the moment. Looking back, they all coalesce to a single calling: To cultivate beauty in defiance of the darkness. On this side of miscarriage, I possess authentic awareness that life will never be only happy. Sad and happy moments simultaneously exist in our lives. There is both genuine beauty and grisly shadow in this world, and to ignore either is dishonest. God invites us not to avoid the darkness but to stare it down, with teary eyes and blood-streaked hands, and say, "You don't own me."

We started a cut flower farm in our backyard in the wake of our loss, and it functions as a tangible incarnation of this calling. Flowers are relatively frail, short-lived splashes of color – like our lives. Yet, they are worth cultivating, arranging, and enjoying. They are worth pondering to hear what the Creator says by making something temporary, intricate, and beautiful.

Ultimately, this is why we grow flowers. It is why we have babies. It is why we seek to invest our lives in the little plot of ground and community of people He has placed us in. It is why we hope: The Creator of Life does not condone Death. He does not give evil that honor. Its effects are tragic, but its weight is empty, finally disarmed at a Cross.

Our tears do not exist just to be wiped away – but they will be. Pain is real, but not initially, nor for eternity. God's telling a much bigger story than death. Therefore, in all that we do, let us remind the darkness that it has already lost.

Wes Spears

The Night I Got Saved

When I was in first grade, a lot of my friends were getting saved and baptized, and I thought, "My dad's the preacher! What will they think of him if I do not get saved?" Of course, I knew all the right words, all the right things and answers to say when questioned about whether I understood, so I went through with it. And every time I was asked about my salvation, that is the story I told because if you tell a story long enough, you begin to believe it, right?

When I was 12 years old, my daddy did a revival in Massachusetts. My parents stayed at my grandmother's house, and my brother and I stayed across the street at grandmother's best friend's house in her spare rooms. I could not sleep one night, so I got up and went to the window to look outside. I was not expecting an answer, but I sort of said, "God, why can't I sleep?" And I have heard people say, "God doesn't speak audibly. It's much louder than that." I heard a voice that said, "Kelli, if you died right now, you would burst hell wide open." And I turned around to see who was in the room with me. It was that clear. Nobody was in the room with me, and I knew, without a shadow of a doubt.

I did not know why I had to have my mom and dad present to be saved, but I wanted them with me. So instead of getting saved right there, I ran to where they were staying across the street. And the funny thing is,

I still remember being extra careful crossing the street because I did not want to die before I asked Jesus into my heart!

I banged on the door and woke them up, and when Daddy answered the door, I said, "Daddy, I need to get saved!" So, he reached for his Bible, but I said, "No! I do not need that; I know it already! I need to get saved right now! Hurry! I need to pray right now!" It was all because of The Voice. I turned around when I heard it, looking to see if someone was in the room with me. It was not a passing thought in my head or my spirit. Maybe it was not out loud. Maybe if someone else were in the room with me, they might not have heard it, but it was out loud for me. I heard it.

Thinking back on it now, the phrase "You would burst hell wide open" may not typically be what God would say to everyone, but as a child, that is a phrase I often heard my daddy use when he was appealing to people to get saved. It was a familiar phrase the Lord knew I would understand immediately, and quite frankly, I am thankful He chose it because that is when I got saved.

Kelli Thomas

Holy Spirit

We are not saved by good work, but by God's work, as Jesus says.

As we walk with our Lord, may we allow His Spirit to speak candidly, be quiet, listen, and follow where he leads.

When God gives an assignment, it comes with His enablement. Acknowledging and knowing God helps us to become what we were meant to be. He will not force His love on us. God's love is a sweet nectar of praise. When in your deepest need, allow the Holy Spirit to speak to you.

God's word is our compass. Please read and follow it. Ask the Holy Spirit to use your words and actions to help and heal, not to throw stones because they just may ricochet.

God's throne is always accessible as you come to Him in prayer. Many Lord, are asking, "Who will bring us prosperity?" Let the light of your face shine on us. God gets the glory.

Edna M. Walker
Edna M. Walker is author of two books -
A Caregiver's Journey Through the Tsunamis of Life and
It's a Heart Thing.

Ignoring God's Voice

When we hear the voice of God, we have a choice. Undivided attention from the Creator of the universe should elicit an automatic positive response, but, alas, we often think we are smarter than God, that we know better. How gracious and merciful He is when we are arrogant, stubborn, and rebellious.

On two distinct occasions in my life, I heard God's voice as clearly as if He had been sitting beside me. Both circumstances were at a serious crossroads in my life and affected my family's journey. I want to share the second experience with you.

Being a left-brained planner, I needed to map out our family's future, whether it was the next day, week, month, year, or decades ahead. My husband was a more in-the-moment guy, so I felt it was up to me to follow Proverbs 29:18: "Where there is no vision, the people perish." In fact, I admonished him with that scripture whenever I wanted my way.

We lived in a small town in Kentucky for the first seven years of our marriage. After the first 14 months, our son was born. Three months later, while traveling in Alabama and Georgia to visit family for Thanksgiving, we were involved in a near-fatal head-on collision. After months of hospitalization, multiple surgeries, and weeks of recovery with relatives, we returned to Kentucky. It was another year before my husband could return to work, but his employer closed the company during that time. During a recession, it was difficult to find employment. However, our amazing friends, neighbors, and church family had become our support group, and we did not want to leave the area.

After our daughter was born, it was clear that we had to make changes to survive financially.

My husband felt we should move back to our home state, but I loved Kentucky and was determined to stay. Although all indicators were that we should move, I found a way to make it happen. My belief that I knew best was leading us down a path of destruction.

My husband was an avid and accomplished tennis player. I discovered a sporting goods franchise that I convinced him we could manage. There were obstacles, and God was obviously trying to put them in front of me, but I was convinced it would work if we "dedicated the business to the Lord." That was a manipulative situation of believing I was smarter than God.

To make a long story short, we did open the franchise. We renovated an old motorcycle shop and had fun decorating and organizing the store. My husband taught tennis clinics and strung racquets, and I managed the business. However, I knew nothing about running a business, we had an established competitor, and the economy was still in recession. We lasted about a year and eventually lost everything. We filed for bankruptcy, sold our house and our collection of lovely antiques, and moved back to Alabama to rent an apartment and start over.

This story, however, is about God's grace and mercy. After the dust settled and we reflected on what went wrong, I heard God say, "I had a plan, but you wanted to do it your way. I am patient and knew the result would be the same, but you just took the long way around." It was a hard lesson, but we repeatedly experienced God's loving-kindness throughout the decades since. I am thankful for His patient guidance and forgiveness when I am defiant and insubordinate, even after clearly hearing His voice.

Sandra Montgomery

Driving to an Answered Prayer

Renting a home and becoming a landlord was never a goal for us, but we moved to Huntsville on a leap of faith, more than a leap. God had spoken to me while I was asleep so profoundly that I knew with confidence that wherever He was taking us, it was going to be okay. It did not happen right away, but three years later, we landed in the Huntsville International Airport, ready to make a new home for our family of five. So, in essence, the leap of faith was to buy a home in Huntsville before selling the home we had left in Michigan. For six months, the house sat empty because the economy had bottomed out, and our neighbors were foreclosing on their homes. It took 12 years for the economy to return to what it was when we left Michigan. God graciously provided renters for all those years.

We decided that it was time to sell our home because the economy had returned to before the market fell out. After spending seven grueling weeks praying over and touching every single inch of the house, doing repairs, replacing flooring, gutting the kitchen, and renovating indoor and outdoor spaces, we finally listed the house, and we were anxious for a buyer. The first offer came just two weeks later, but it fell through because of the inspection results. The requested repairs were great for a half-century home, even though we had worked so hard. Back on this fair market, we waited anxiously for what God had in mind. It was about six weeks listed when my agent produced a new offer, a full-price offer with no contingencies, except to pass inspection. Of course, we accepted the offer and prayed. Our hard work had paid off, but we would have to be patient about the inspection because it was a holiday weekend.

As we drove the children to school the following week, our youngest son, Grayson, who was twelve, closed the daily devotional, and I asked him if he would pray for our day. Without hesitation, he asked, "What should I pray for, Mom?" Naturally, my list included what was weighing heavily on my heart, the inspection. Obediently, he did as I asked, and I simultaneously was silently praying because I knew this was more than a teaching moment but an opportunity for his faith to grow too. Feeling anxious, I gripped the steering wheel a little tighter. I was crossing the Monte Sano light at the top of Governors Drive when I heard my phone chime. A text arrived on my phone about one minute after his prayer, so I asked Grayson to check my phone just in case there was an emergency. It was about 7:30 am and the only person I was expecting at that time of day was my husband. To my surprise, Grayson read aloud, "It's Andrea (our realtor), and she said that there would not be an inspection." Leaning in a little closer while staying focused on the road, I asked him to repeat himself and double-check that what he read was correct, but nothing was different the second time around. "That cannot be right; please call her," I urged him, but he only got her voicemail. I sat back in my seat, feeling puzzled until I realized that God had just answered Grayson's prayer while we were driving. My heart soared, knowing that he was experiencing one of his first answered prayers--a double blessing.

Fast forward to our closing. The woman who bought our home seemed like she would explode if she did not get something out. Excitedly, she told us how she had planned to purchase a different home, but in short, she walked away from it. Finding our home was an answer to her prayers. She claimed that her new home was perfect for her and that every detail, from the color choices to the French drain in the basement, was as if she had personally made them herself.

God orchestrated every detail for her story and ours, and the details do not end there, but most importantly, Grayson experienced God in a very tangible way, and so did we. The best is yet to come!

Angela Hawke

Homelessness

In her classic, "Tell Me the Story of Jesus," the famous hymnist Fanny Crosby described Jesus as "homeless, rejected, and poor." In all my years of singing that hymn in my grandparents' church, that line in the second stanza never caught my attention. Reading it as an adult, however, was jarring. Could Jesus really have been homeless? As I pondered the question, a piece of Scripture came to mind in which Jesus encounters a man desiring to follow him. Jesus responds by telling him that foxes have dens and birds have nests, but the Son of

Man has no place to lay his head. While no one can say for sure if Jesus actually experienced homelessness on earth, no one can say he does not deeply empathize with those who do. Jesus knows and perhaps experienced the plight of the poor.

In his sermon on the mount, Jesus spoke not of the material wealth to build an earthly kingdom but of spiritual wealth designed to bring the Kingdom of God to earth. "Blessed are the poor in spirit, for theirs is the kingdom of heaven," he began. "Blessed are the meek, the merciful, those who hunger and thirst for righteousness," He continued. Those physical descriptors of hunger and thirst to describe spiritual fulfillment nearly bring me to tears each time I read them. I believe that is why many who experience homelessness can speak of God as a friend. They know what it means to hunger and thirst, and they know the peace of experiencing God as closer than a brother.

This was the case with Zeke. I was working from the church office one afternoon, which was in the back of a shared building with several businesses. A lady from the printing business that used the front of the space stepped back to let me know a gentleman was there to see me. As I walked to the front with her, she let me know he looked homeless. This was not surprising because our building was within walking distance of a homeless camp, and several people from that camp had been attending church with us.

I stepped out onto the portico where an older black gentleman with peppered hair stuck out his hand. "Hi. My name's Ezekiel." He had the presence of a prophet, so the name was fitting. He smiled with his whole face. As I shook his hand, I looked into his steely eyes, which seemed to lead straight into his soul. He went on to tell me he needed his medicine to combat a heart disorder. I pointed him in the right direction to receive the help he needed, but I knew I had met a friend that day.

Ray lived in the same camp as Zeke. Ray had begun attending our church in the early days when we set up and tore down our chairs and equipment in the storefront. Ray showed up early each Sunday and helped us out when he felt like it. You could not help but love Ray, and he probably loved you back, but no one could be certain. Ray would call me once every few weeks to let me know he was hungry. "What's for breakfast?" he would ask immediately. His usual phone calls were quite humorous, if not endearing, but there is one call, an unusual one, that I will never forget.

 It was early one December morning, unusually early for Ray to call. With a shaking voice, he let me know Zeke died during the night. I arrived at the camp just after the police came onto the scene. I found Ray, hugged him, and then watched as the officers dragged Zeke out of his tent, feet first. His heart gave up on him sometime in the night, and it broke my heart as I watched them place his body in a bright blue bag. Days later, many of

Zeke's friends gathered at that same camp to eat, laugh, and share stories. Zeke had pointed so many to Jesus throughout his life. And while the hope is that each of us, like Zeke, will spend eternity in heaven, I believe we should spend our lives bringing heaven to Earth.

Chase Allen

Following The Voice

"My sheep hear my voice, and I know them, and they follow me." John 10:27. God speaks specifically to the plans HE has for us, how those plans are carried out, and the necessary resources to accomplish the task. However, we must be willing, prepared to listen, and prepared to go wherever HIS voice leads and follow the voice of GOD before what needs to be accomplished can be accomplished. Following HIS voice means obeying HIS voice. And if you are like me, obeying something blindly or without faith, not knowing the actual outcome does not readily happen. Looking back over my life, visualizing going down Avenue A when His voice clearly instructed me to go down Avenue Z. My rationale was that my way would take me less time to get there, so I ignored the voice. Or choosing door number three instead of door number nine because it was my favorite color. Again, we cannot only hear HIS voice. We must be prepared to act, never wavering, when we hear it.

For the first time in my adult Christian life, I not only heard the voice of the Lord but obeyed it. It was as if HE were sitting right next to me and telling me to start packing my belongings, to quit my job, and then nothing, silence. Now not being Abraham, I did not respond right away. Procrastination overshadowed me, leading me to forget the instructions for a period. "Where will I go?" and "What am I going to do?" were the million-dollar questions when I finally gave ear to HIS prompting. I will need a job, a way to take care of myself, and a place to stay. COVID-19 became our reality, so days turned into weeks and weeks into months before the job of preparing for whatever was to come next was completed. It took me more than one and a half years to finish what I had been instructed by His voice to do. I relocated to Pine Bluff, Arkansas, as the primary caregiver to my aging, desperately ill parents. I was utterly unprepared for what would meet me there. Of course, I knew it would not be a walk in the park, but I did not know my whole world would be transformed from footloose and fancy-free, doing what I wanted to do when I wanted to do it, to now being relegated to the house almost nonstop with the same routine each day. My life was no longer my own. It was controlled by my new reality--CAREGIVER. As a caregiver, there was a range of emotions. Emotionally, I experienced the loss of self, loss of my job and consistent income, loss of control, and loss of a sense of independence. There were also emotions such as resentment because my life is no longer my own, anger due to taking on this role without respite, guilt for feeling angry or resentful. After all, these are my parents. These should not be my feelings. Worry about my future because I am not too far from retirement. But then, I began to understand that GOD had not made a mistake in taking me on this journey, that from it, there would be more blessings than not. A greater work and, more importantly, the kingdom would be much better suited for me.

Quitting my job, leaving my comfort zone, venturing into the unknown of being a caregiver, none of which promoted me to sainthood automatically installed a halo atop my head, nor did it guarantee my entrance into the kingdom. However, feelings that I never knew I could feel or existed surfaced, mainly because those I would be caring for were my parents, that I felt embarrassed for this behavior. Feelings that would not have garnered acceptance into the kingdom. But it also allowed me to view my parents through a vastly different lens. I not only knew of my parents, but I also began to know my parents. I discovered that my parents had doubts, insecurities, regrets, and fears. Had they done the best they could in raising their children using the resources given to them at that time? That if it were possible, they would "do-over" their lives. Most of us probably would. They would spend more time enjoying life, traveling, enjoying, and spending time with one another, Not sweating the small stuff, knowing it is all small stuff. That acceptance, forgiveness, and forgetting are essential attributes in life. Time or space will allow me to continue what seems to be an exhaustive list of discoveries. I was in awe at all that was and continues to be uncovered.

"Wisdom is gained from listening to the voice. Blessings come because of obeying what you hear from the voice" (The Diocese of Lagos--Listening to God's Voice). I am so happy that I listened.

The saga continues as I still wear the hat of caregiver to both parents. It will be interesting to see how GOD's plan will be manifested in my life. I eagerly await HIS voice.

Carol Boyd

When Purpose and Hope are Lost

Hope is a simple four-letter word that can be given or lost. A few years ago, I lost my purpose and, I guess, my hope.

My children had grown up and started their independent lives, my husband traveled for work, and I woke up thinking, what is my purpose? I could not think of one thing at that dark moment even though I had a lovely home, plenty of food, and money in the bank. I left my house with my car, driver's license, and some pocket change. I had no idea what I was going to do or where I was going.

The journey became an awakening. For ten days, I drove through states, having no plan and feeling just numb. I slept in my car and drank water from any source I could find. I felt like I was homeless, even though I could not blend in with all the homeless since they seemed to be invisible.

I ended my journey after I ran out of gas at a shelter for homeless, battered women. They knew I was not battered but just needed to rest. There I was assigned a simple room and a cabinet in the kitchen with nothing but generic boxes. It was that moment that started to turn my life around. I thought, "Is this how we treat people who seem to have no hope, like generic human beings? Does anybody care?"

My caretaking instinct took over, and I started to find a purpose there. I started cooking for the two women who were there. One woman landed on my heart. She was about 65 years old and had her back broken several times from bad relationships. She had no home, family, or hope. I cooked, we ate in silence, and I told them I would even clean up. While I was putting the dishes away in the cabinet, my hand slipped on the door, and it slammed. The 65-year-old woman jumped and was scared. I apologized profusely, and with tears in her eyes, she said, "Nobody has ever said they were sorry to me." "Wow!" was all I could say. How sad of me to think so low of me. I had never had to experience that emotion. I knew at that moment what one of my purposes would be. I would serve, no matter the circumstance, and spread hope where I could.

This is one of the reasons that Community of Hope is so important to me. All human beings need hope and purpose.

Diana Henry - WAY FM.

GO!

Two letters. A small word. Big impact. In March 2010, I walked from my bedroom to my office. I was home alone. My goal that day was to load the dishwasher. You see, in October of 2009, I had mentally crashed. I was determined that I did not need my depression medicine. Boy, was I wrong. I heard the word "Go." Nothing else.

Just go. It was not a scream, but it was not a whisper either. It was direct and to the point. I immediately picked up the phone and called Roger Jones, my district commissioner. To understand, I need to take you back a couple of years.

In 2007, I had young boys, 7 and 3. I lived in NE Huntsville and my boys wanted to play at the Community-Built playground in South Huntsville because it was HUGE and much better than anything on our side of town. This was when God started putting it on my heart that we needed a playground like this on our side in the city. I remember visiting the Airport Road playground and saying out loud, "We need something like this on our side of town." I had spoken it out loud. I remember telling my husband, "We need this on our side of town, and Sharon Johnston Park would be a great place for it." I had spoken it out loud. I wanted it and saw a need for it, but I certainly was not anticipating what God had for me next.

Now you are caught up to March 2010 and the phone call to Commissioner Jones. I told him my idea. We talked for a few minutes, and then he contacted another person who put a meeting on the calendar.

I felt God wanted me to do a Community Built Playground. The community raised the money and physically built the playground. At the time, I thought they would take better care of it because the community felt ownership of it. That is true, but I feel like it did much more. It brought people together to work towards a common goal, making relationships. It was a big, challenging task. You could find me in my bedroom closet, crying many days and asking God why He had me doing this. I had no experience in ANY of the things that needed to be done to complete this task. God brought together an average group of people to perform this amazing job, like the twelve disciples. It is now 2021, and the playground is ten years old. I am still honored that God allowed me to help give my community His gift. I do not typically hear God talk audibly. But that day, He did, and I am glad I listened.

Kristina Bass

Flood of Grace

On February 23, 2019, my family and I were awakened by firefighters ringing our doorbell just before dawn. They were on a mission to notify our neighborhood of an unexpected and rapidly deteriorating situation. An ocean of water was building in my neighborhood while we slept peacefully. With shock and disbelief, we got dressed and began assessing what we needed to do. The firefighters advised us to leave, and it would have to be by boat. I had only witnessed such a catastrophic scene on TV. All the city officials called it "A Hundred Year Flood," the likes none of us had ever experienced.

Strangers, neighbors, and friends gathered in wading boots, trying to sandbag and help each other salvage what was possible. The forecast called for storms and even more substantial rainfall totals. I packed boxes and moved things off the floor, hoping to save as many mementos as I could.

I called my best friend with panic echoing through my voice, insisting that everything looked hopeless. There was no way my home could avoid this devastation because my garage and patio were already underwater. Just a few inches more, and the house would be too. My friend is gifted in hearing and recognizing God's voice right away. She confidently and sweetly refuted what I had just told her. She proclaimed that it was God's house, and the water would stop wherever He said it to. Clinging to this new realization and hope, I agreed. My daughter stood teary-eyed in the doorway, watching the waters continue to rise. I spoke to her the same words as we joined hands and prayed aloud, thanking God for His protection for us and over our home. Scripture began to flood my mind as we prayed. We wrote Isaiah 43:1-2 on our chalkboard hanging in our kitchen. We took the boat and went to stay with family.

The flooding of our area made local news channels. The outcome looked bleak. The following morning, we were allowed to wade in waist-high water back into our neighborhood. It looked like a warzone. The devastation was etched on our neighbors' faces. Upon entering our house, we were astounded to see our home spared. We stood in disbelief but relieved with gratitude. I felt guilty that all my surrounding neighbors were hurting so badly, and my life would continue as normal while they lived in hotels during their homes' reconstruction.

I took everything while reflecting on all that had happened the previous month with my family. My sister had suffered a major heart attack in January, requiring open-heart surgery with some complications. I was already emotionally and mentally drained from worry. God knows what is going to happen and all that we cannot foresee. He knew where I had been and what lay ahead. Three weeks after the floods ravaged our neighborhood, I found out my marriage of twenty-three years was over.

This time I was the one who was devastated by a different kind of storm that came without warning. I was not prepared. Isaiah 43:1-2 washed over my soul repeatedly again. I know God had saved my home for my daughter and me, and I knew He would restore me and would be with us through all that lay ahead.

My daughter and I know our home belongs to Him. It is a happy home, fully restored with laughter, peace, and love. We are safe here. I pray that my daughter always remembers the day she and I joined hands and prayed and how God miraculously kept the waters back, even though it did not make sense. I pray she feels lavished in His love and sees there is always hope when we turn to Him. He goes before us, whether it is through rain, sunshine, laughter, or tears.

"... Fear not for I have redeemed you; I have summoned you by name; you are mine. When you pass through the waters, I will be with you; and when you pass through the rivers, they will not sweep over you. When you walk through the fire, you will not be burned; the flames will not set you ablaze." Isaiah 43:1-2

Beth Brown

The Importance of Baptism

All the years I have worked, and all the people I have worked with, this gentleman, Jim, was a straight-up person, a no-nonsense person, if I may say. He was raised Catholic, his wife Mary was raised Catholic, and he and Mary raised their family in the Catholic religion. Over the nearly 30 years, Jim and I would talk about JESUS, prophecy, and present truths. I remember many times talking to him about the world conditions throughout the years. We would always say there was not much time left before JESUS returned.

In August of 2020, I woke up one morning, and immediately, a still, small voice told me to call Jim and tell him, not ask him, that he and Mary need to be baptized. It was not a matter of maybe but must be baptized. I thank the LORD that I listened to that voice. I am getting weak and choked up as I write this, knowing I could have brushed this aside and not heard the LORD speaking to me. Immediately, I called Jim and told him he must be baptized and Mary as well. Remember that Jim and I have never talked or hinted about him or Mary getting baptized before. But this morning was the call I will never forget. When I mentioned to Him about getting baptized, he immediately said yes. I got chills at that moment, and I told Him he must tell Mary about getting baptized. She said she would think about it, and the next day, she responded to Jim, and Jim told me she had said yes. I was extremely excited. Remember, throughout the years, Jim and I have had like a 30-year Bible study. Jim and Mary saying yes reminded me of the Eunuch story in Acts 8, especially verses 36-38. In verse thirty-six, the Eunuch asks, "What hinders me from being baptized?" In verse thirty-seven, Philip tells him, "...If thou believest with all thine heart, thou mayest." And he answered and said those golden words, "I believe that Jesus Christ is the Son of God." And in verse thirty-eight, they both went into the water, and the Eunuch was baptized. This reminded me of that story because I specifically asked them both that very same question, and they had said "Yes." One month later, in September of 2020, both Jim and Mary were baptized. The story does not end here. Two months after Jim and Mary got back home, they both contracted Covid-19. Mary contracted it first, then a week and a half later, Jim tested positive for the disease. After two weeks of Covid-19, Mary was able, through the grace of God, to get through it. However, Jim had to be hospitalized. He would tell me how much he witnessed people in the hospital, even though he was sick. In those last days, he could not see Mary, only talk to her. I talked to him either by voice or text. Sometimes, he was so weak that he could not breathe and would get out of breath from talking. He continued to get worse until, after 50 days of being in the hospital, he died. I thank God for that small, tiny voice giving me instructions for Jim and that he and his wife had taken heed to GOD speaking to them through me. And as I am writing this story, I am reminded of Mark 16:16, "He that believeth and is baptized shall be saved; but he that believeth not shall be damned." Only GOD knows the future. He knew Jim, He knew his heart, and He prepared him to receive HIM wholeheartedly. While it is a sad time because he is not with us today, it will be a glorious and happy time when JESUS returns because I honestly believe Jim will be counted in that number going back to Paradise.

James Burch

Dear Clifford,

In response to my longing, in 1984, to love and feel loved completely by another person, God said to me, "No, Freddie, not until you are satisfied, fulfilled and content with being loved by me alone."

For one year I experienced an intensely personal and unique relationship with God. I united with Him exclusive of anyone or anything else, exclusive of any desires or longings.

God also said, "Even if you are ready, I'll surprise you with a love far more wonderful than you dreamed of." And honey, that love was you. God brought the new Clifford Harris into existence just for me.

When you gave me one red rose that Saturday evening 10 years ago, the Holy Spirit impressed me with the words, "He's the one," and (not knowing He had said 'she's the one' to you earlier that same day. And I still hear the words ringing in my ears from my oldest son, saying in response to your interest in me, "Mommy, if there is any man, I'd like to see you marry, it's him." I knew that the Holy Spirit impressed him as He did me.

On Sunday, the very next day, you asked me to marry you and I immediately said, "Yes." Having spent one intense year with God, I knew He had chosen you for my husband. What a miracle!

On May 11, 1995, my Father led me to my list of 16-character traits that I had specifically requested for in my husband. The list was dated 04-28-84 (we were married 05-10-85) and every request on the list God granted me, including pretty feet (smile!). He is wonderful! And He is just that personal.

God designed a two-fold purpose for our lives, marriage, and the birth of the Drug Alternative Program. What miracles He has performed, not only in our marriage, but also with DAP. We've both committed to do this work until Jesus comes. No retirement!

On this our 10th wedding anniversary and my pending 50th birthday (June 2) celebration, I want to say, "Honey, thank you for making me the happiest woman in the entire world. I love you and Jesus loves you even more!"

Your "One Red Rose,"

Freddie
(Reprint from book "Yours, Truly" – One Women's Conversation with God; page 209, by Freddie Harris.)

Who Will Take Care of Me?

I am the oldest of three siblings. Both preceded me to be with the Lord. My mother was the first to depart before them.

I have three (3) children, six (6) grandchildren, and eight (8) great-grandchildren.

They all reside in various states with their families, and I live alone in another.

For all my life, I have taken care of them in some capacity.

In recent years, it seems I have had one surgery after another. I was afraid and nervous during those times because none of my family members could be with me during my times of need for one reason or another.

Tearfully, I remember praying and asking God, "Who will take care of me?"

And it was almost a whisper when I heard Him say, "I will."

That "whisper" restored my "Faith." Amen.

Janis Ruffin

The Voice of the Lord, the Path to Life

I am an achiever. In my life, I had always been able to "take things on" to see something I wanted to do or felt needed to be done and do it. Not only would I get it done, but others would praise me for doing it well. Continuous achievement was my idol, and the resulting praises and successes were my prizes. That worked well until life's responsibilities and commitments overtook the allotted time in a day. My pursuit of achievement and the over-pursuit of the Lord and His will for my life was about to catch up with me in a painful way. Now I see the experience as the extreme grace of the Lord in my life.

I attended River tree Church for about six months when a Men's Retreat weekend came around in October 2018. It was a good two days of teaching and fellowship, and the culminating assignment was to be alone with the Lord for one hour. Attendees were to leave their phones in the car or at the church and find a secluded spot where they would not be bothered. Once private, they were to pray to the Lord, asking Him to speak into their lives, then be still and listen for a word from Him. I went to a nature preserve, walked into the woods, prayed, then sat by a stream. It was...weird. For a while, I felt like I was just talking to the air and that this would be a fruitless endeavor. I pleaded with the Lord some more and eventually had three thoughts (the voice of the Lord) pass through my mind: 1 – "Create space," 2- "Love your wife," 3 – "Keep doing this." I wrote them down, then went back to the retreat and discussed them with my small group.

I thought of specific actions based on what God had given me. First, I needed to stop all the youth sports coaching I pursued and stop overcommitting at work. Those two actions would "create space" in my life to focus on the essential things rather than the urgent ones. The following two thoughts were dependent on the first. I needed to focus on my relationship with my wife, a true gift from the Lord in my life. My pursuit of career and extracurricular achievement left little to no time for our relationship and a healthy home life with my kids. Finally, I needed to "keep doing this." "This" means devoting significant time alone with the Lord in prayer, study, and worship to commune regularly with the only life-giving relationship available, my relationship with Jesus Christ. I left the weekend with these thoughts in mind, and then I went back to life and implemented NONE of it.

In spring 2019, I started having panic attacks. There was so much happening in life, and I could not keep up. Why couldn't I get it done and to my standards? I needed to try harder, do more. My wife was upset with me... Does she not see how hard I am working? My work constantly praised me, but I felt that what I was "supposed" to achieve was not getting done. I compare my weaknesses to the strengths of people God gifted differently than me. I do not deserve to be where I am. Random days, more and more often, I just must walk outside and cry. What is wrong with me?

In July 2019, we had just bought a new home. My wife and I were working on a few projects before we completely moved in. I received a call from my mom. My brother-in-law (one of my closest friends) was in a coma from anaphylactic shock after accidentally disturbing a yellow jacket nest. I drove to be with my family. I held my sister by his bedside as he went in and out of cardiac arrest. He did not make it, despite the immense efforts of the ER team, despite our pleas to God, despite him being maybe the best person I know. It was time for Jacob to go. Why? There is no time to grieve with the many people around me who need me. They need to grieve. I must support them. I do. It hurts. Funeral arrangements, coordinating with friends, fielding calls about the accident, death certificates, financial arrangements, endless conversations take a lot of time.

In the fall/winter of 2019, things settled down. I was back at work and working back towards "normalcy" after the most traumatic event of my life. Something was off in a worse way than before. I still have bouts with anxiety, but now I am almost unable to function as my typical self. It is like the trauma I had just gone through exposed the underlying voids in my heart, ones that only Jesus can fill. I finally broke and decided to go back to the first thing the Lord had told me to do--"create space... I backed away from coaching sports and informed my employer that I would be intentionally stepping out of leadership roles for a while. All parties are gracious to me, but I still am just "off." Every conversation feels awkward. I think I am depressed. It gets dark. I often do not want to start the day.

It was 2020. Depression has taught me something. My idol of achievement, my prizes of success and praise... those things make for terrible Gods. Without the Lord at the center of our lives, even the pursuit of "good" things leads to death. Through the grace and love of the Lord, the people He put in my life (my wife, numerous friends, and family), and surrender to His lordship over my life, I began feeling restoration. COVID hit and further helped me continue "creating space," and I devoted myself more and more to spending time with Jesus and his Word. I connected more with my wife and brothers in Christ than I ever had, and all I can say is that the Lord completely redeemed me. My awkwardness and anxiety disappeared, and I found a new level of peace and confidence in life. I felt like I was moving forward again, though now I know any achievements worked through me from the Lord. (John 15:1-8). He prepared any works that I partake in, and it is only those that mean anything. Life is sweet when you realize that you do not have to achieve perfection because Christ's perfection covers you. When you know that His blood covers inevitable mistakes, disappointments, and setbacks and that he will continue His good work in you. Rest in the truth that Jesus's plan for our lives is better than anything we design for ourselves.

I praise God for his voice directing me to create space in my life in 2018, even though it took a painful correction for me to implement. His discipline in my life was an act of love, as my pursuit of the world led to death. The Word of the Lord tells us in Psalm 34:8, "Oh, taste and see that the LORD is good! Blessed is the man who takes refuge in him!" I encourage anyone reading this to pursue the Lord over all else in their lives. In Him alone will you find refuge and be blessed! I leave you with a poem I wrote recently regarding the importance of laying down your "Daily Yes" to the will of the Father.

Joseph P. Holland

Daily Yes

My Christ, my life, the one and only Way.
Beside still waters, You lead me each day.
Yet my flesh still chases the world's false hopes.
Kill it, I must, or be left on the ropes.
If I do not, the waters get rough.

We are not promised a life of ease, but peace when things get tough.

This promise has conditions though; are there things we must do?

Well, kind of. It is hard to explain, but it is not really on you.

All that He asks, to experience the fruit,
Is to lay down your "yes" to Him, and to the things He is prepared for you.

When you give him your "yes," He gives you the words.
These works are not yours, but His, the One who feeds even the birds.

He values the birds but loves us much more.
What we need from Him, we get. So be warned if you run from His door.

So, say "yes" to Lord Jesus. Say "yes" to His ways!

Destroy your old flesh and find Life each and every day!

By: Joseph P. Holland

Give It to God

Let me tell you of a great blessing I once received to let you know the power of our Lord when we allow Him into our lives.

How often have you said, "I'm going to give this to God?" I know I have, many times. But just how often have we? When we give our problems to Him, we no longer worry because we know God has the situation well in hand, and His will be done.

But instead, we often end up worrying, wringing our hands, pacing the floor, and still carrying the very thing we said we would give to God. Well, one time, I felt I needed the Lord so badly that if I had never truly given my troubles to God, now was the time.

In 1998, someone stabbed my youngest son, and the wound was so deep that it penetrated his small intestines clean through to his liver. This wound bled profusely, and I knew that the only way my son would survive would be through the grace of God. When I arrived at the hospital, my son was in a bed with a huge towel folded on his stomach, drenched in blood. Laying there with his feet shaking back and forth, he said to me, "I am going to be alright, Mom." I walked up to him, placed my hand on his forehead, and I began to pray. I prayed, "Lord, pass through me as I touched my son and heal him as only you can."

As I was praying, I heard the Lord say, "Be still and wait on me." As I said, "Amen," the surgeon entered the room, told us they were taking him to surgery and showed us to the waiting room. As I waited for some word, my family started arriving. Some were sobbing, others angry, and all were full of questions. I could not go down the paths they were traveling. I had to hold steadfast to what the Lord had told me--to be still and wait on Him. So, I said, "If you want to help him, please go to the chapel and pray." Then I sat as far away from the family, asking questions, and crying, and I shut down.

I was so afraid that if I would say I hope, I wish, or anything that meant I had not given the situation to God, I would lose my son. After what seemed to be an eternity, but only about two hours, the surgeon came in and said, "I don't know how after losing so much blood, he is awake, sitting up, and asking for his mother?" Before I could run to his room, which I did, I had to tell the surgeon, "I don't know what you did in the operating room, but this was all through the goodness of our Lord and Savior."

My son is now forty-six, has three adult children and a granddaughter. Every day, I thank my Heavenly Father for sparing his life. To God be the Glory! Amen.

Pamela North

All Things Work Together for Good

The Holy Spirit spoke to me through the trials of my adult children, thus teaching me how my Savior brings lessons of self-denial into my life.

When certain situations happened to my children, I felt as though it was happening to me. When one was rejected by a spouse and left to live alone to go through separation and divorce, I experienced the situation from my fears. My feelings of rejection, my sense of "what's going to happen next?" The feeling of helplessness was overwhelming, as if it were happening to me, me, and I! I wondered how a supposed Christian could do this to my child. Why would God let this happen to an offspring of mine?

But then, after much prayer and agonizing with the Lord, the Holy Spirit moved slowly but surely in eye-opening ways to let me know this situation was not about me. He let me see that He was with my child, and if I would just call on Him, give it all to Him in prayer, which I certainly did, then He would work it all out for her good.

I lived, loved, and learned that what God said was indeed true: "Now He who searches the hearts knows what the mind of the Spirit is because He makes intercession.... according to the will of God. And we know that all things work together for good to those who love God, to those who are called according to His purpose. Roman 8:27, 28

Carol Byars

The Miracle

I have considered myself a Christian since I was in the seventh grade and attended the youth group at the local church.

The Lord has helped me through a divorce after 20 years of marriage, leaving me, a stay-at-home-mom, with three children to raise. Several years later, I remarried, and after 28 years together, I lost that husband to cancer. After his death, I sold everything we owned in Michigan, moved to Florida, and stayed there in our winter home. Being a Christian, I needed to find a new church home, so I visited several and decided on New Walk. The General Baptist denomination sponsors the New Walk Church. Their philosophy is that to maintain spiritual health and strength, three essential elements are needed to be in place in every Christian's life: worship, small group study, and service.

I loved the music (a live band), and the pastor seemed to speak the message directly to me each Sunday. One Sunday morning, the message was "What Voices Do You Hear?" I experienced some burning and discomfort in the middle of my chest. I was scheduled for a routine appointment with my cardiologist, and I kept hearing this voice in my head telling me that I should mention this to the doctor. I was on medication and had been for over a year for Acid Reflux, but the symptoms did not go away; in fact, they were getting worse. After mentioning my discomfort to the doctor, I was scheduled for a Stress Test, which I failed. Next, I was scheduled for a Heart Cath. which showed my heart was fine. I did not have any blockages. But the doctor saw a minor seepage of blood, and he was afraid of blood clots, so he decided to keep me overnight in the hospital. He ordered a Ct. Angiogram of the Heart to discover that I had a 6.5-centimeter aneurysm in my Aorta that put me in an urgent status for Open Heart Surgery which took place six days later.

I had to have a whole New Valve Replacement, a very delicate surgery, and I was on the table for 7 hours. I am now known in my cardiologist's office as "the miracle." My cardiologist and the surgeon both said it was just a fluke and that they had found the aneurysm.

Without the Lord Jesus and his steady voice prompting me to seek medical attention, I would not be here writing my testimony. "I consider my life worth nothing to me, if only I can finish the race and complete the task the Lord Jesus has given me--the task of testifying to the gospel of God's grace." Acts 20:24

Sharon Sinift

Mountains Speak to Me

Just 20 years before my arrival on Okinawa, up to one-third of the island's population had been killed in battles fought there during WWII, between Japan and the United States. Okinawans generally blamed the American military for these deaths, and some had a deep disdain for Americans, especially the military.

However, relations between Okinawans and Americans were quite different at the local Seventh-day Adventist Okinawa Medical Mission facility (OMM). I attribute much of this to what I call the "Desmond Doss Effect." Even in combat, US Army Medic Pvt. Doss showed love for wounded enemies. It was reported that he had even given medical supplies and assistance to OMM while on the Island. The bonds he established created a warm, loving, accepting atmosphere at OMM for Americans two decades later. His life epitomized true Christianity. For several decades, OMM was revered as the best place on the Island to go for kind, quality medical care.

While serving at the US Army Medical Center, I became familiar with the Battle of Okinawa and heard various accounts from local survivors of the war. I even heard Pastor Arikaki's version from a Japanese Army's perspective and how the life of Pvt greatly impacted him. Doss.

One summer afternoon, Pastor Arikaki and several nurses from OMM took a few American soldiers and me on a tour of the famed Maeda Escarpment, later nicknamed "Hacksaw Ridge." This was the place where, on May 21, 1945, after his commanding officers ordered a retreat and surrounded by enemy soldiers, Pvt. Doss went alone into the battle fray and rescued seventy-five of his wounded comrades.

On the Maeda Escarpment, I wandered away from the group to a quiet spot and paused for a reflective moment. Silently, the words of the poem, "Mountains Speak to Me," captured my mind. "Mountains, mountains, mountains speak to me? I've been told, and I believe mountains know it all." I concluded that no single medic could have accomplished such an extraordinary feat without divine intervention.

Fifty years later, I picture Mel Gibson standing on the Maeda Escarpment. He meditates for a moment, then poses the same question as I had. "Mountains, mountains, mountains speak to me? I've been told and I believe mountains know it all."

His result was HACKSAW RIDGE! It was a powerful film, an Academy Award contender, and a classic. It was hailed as one of the best war movies of all time. A God-story about Desmond Doss, a Christian young man who heard and followed the voice, inspired millions worldwide.

Michael Sales

God's Vision for Me

This all started in 2011 when I decided to attend graduate school at Alabama A&M University. I had previously left my first job out of college working for the Mayor of Birmingham, the late Larry Langford, as his Communications Officer. After leaving this job, which was good initially but became depressing as I got into day-to-day politics, I moved to Huntsville to be with my now wife Crystal and our first daughter Sa 'Nya. I luckily got a job at the Space and Rocket Center as a Crew Trainer. Knowing that I did not want to do this long-term, I applied to the graduate Social Work program at AAMU for Social Work.

This is when divine intervention first began to introduce itself. I was blessed to have an internship opportunity at American Senior Assistance Program (ASAP), a geriatric care management company owned by Chanda Crutcher. If you ever get to meet Chanda, you will know the type of mentorship I received while at ASAP. She really helped me to become comfortable with being myself and, at the same time, be an effective social worker. Chanda enabled me to use my gifts to help others. She is by far one of the most influential people I have come across in my life. After the internship, Chanda informed me of a pilot program initiated by a local state agency TARCOG and encouraged me to apply. Honestly, at first, I was kind of hurt because I loved working for Chanda, and I really enjoyed being a part of the team and working with my clients. However, Chanda really insisted this could be an excellent opportunity for me, especially with graduation right around the corner. So, I began my research on this pilot program.

This program turned out to be the Community Care Transitions Program, a pilot program started by CMS to lower the readmissions of their Medicare patients all over the nation. This team was responsible for the Medicare patients discharged from hospitals in TARCOG's coverage area, Huntsville Hospital being one. I applied and was selected to be one of the first five people hired to start this program here in Huntsville. I can remember like it was yesterday. My first day was on my birthday in 2013. As we went through orientation, they informed us that we would be traveling to Denver for training. We were all excited. We then went to Denver for training to be Transitional Care Coaches. The training was excellent, and I learned a lot. We returned ready to help patients remain out of the hospital while living healthier lives. We were good at it too. We were one of the top teams in the nation, but CMS felt it was time to end the program, and they notified us that the program would be coming to an end. This devastated me because I loved my job and enjoyed helping patients live better. All I could think about was what I could do to keep this going. This was when God blessed me with a vision. I took that vision, illustrated it through a business plan, and presented it to physicians and case management organizations all over Huntsville. Most of them said no, and the others gave me a weak maybe. I was beginning to feel defeated until God opened a door.

The former Director of Case Management at Huntsville, Brenda Brooks, knew of my mission of continuing this program because not only was she the first person I presented to, but she also saw the benefits firsthand being that we service her patients. She introduced me to LHC Group who has a joint venture with Huntsville Hospital. I presented my program to them, and the rest is history!!!

In 2017, I started as a Transitional Care Coach Program at Huntsville Hospital. I have two other coaches that came along with me from TARCOG: Helen Shepherd and Treena Waters. The companionship that my team possesses is nothing less than a blessing. Together, we have helped thousands of patients that have been discharged from Huntsville Hospital. By assisting patients in finding primary care physicians, obtaining medications that have been prescribed, transportation to physician visits, and whatever is necessary to enhance their quality of life. The divine thing about my story is that not only did God bless me with a vision, but He strategically placed extraordinary people on my path to help inspire, motivate, and mentor me when I wanted to give up or was feeling defeated. It was nothing else but God that could make something like this become a reality.

By: Akeem J. Davis

Hearing the Voice say I am Enough

For me, "hearing" God's voice has never been an audible one. It has been a deep knowing, a certainty I cannot explain. His calling always lines up with scripture, and He always supplies what is needed to fulfill the calling. That does not mean the journey will be easy, but He does promise "He is enough." Mom was a good mom, and she loved her family. Her family was a priority before the drinking became all-consuming, followed closely by holiday traditions and Alabama football.

Mom came from a family of addicts. She grew up with an alcoholic father and mother, and she was not the only sibling to battle addiction. She grew up quickly, always caring for someone. She loved being "motherly." As the oldest of five children, she helped care for her siblings. At 18, she met and married my father. At 19, she had me. Her 12-year-old baby sister, Angie, came to live with us when I was five. I had a sister stillborn at birth when I was six. Then my little sister, Sandi, came along when I was nine.

Mom never wanted to be an alcoholic, but her drinking had begun to consume more and more of her life. I was losing my mom. It was a slow and excruciating process for all of us.

About ten years ago, the hurt caused by my mom's alcoholism was overwhelming. I wanted to walk away.

Every broken promise, every lie, every missed event, and near-death experience had all taken their toll on me. Mom had hit bottom a dozen times and had gone through more rehabs than I can count. Things only got worse. I began begging God to let me walk away. I sought scripture and counsel from other Christians. I needed someone to show me in God's Word where I could cut off the relationship and let her go. The pain was too deep, and it was never-ending. Even though I found loving people who told me it was okay to walk away, I could not find anything in scripture giving me approval.

My heart was heavy, and my spirit restless. Honestly, I knew God was calling me into deeper waters, but I was resisting. In searching God's Word for permission to walk away, I was constantly reminded of God's unconditional love for His children (1 John 4:15, Eph 2:8, Jeremiah 31:3, John 3:16). His love is steadfast in our brokenness. I was also reminded that I am to take up my cross and follow Him. I am called to love as Jesus loves unconditionally and allow Him to love others through my brokenness. Finally, I bowed my head, dropped my will, and said, "Yes." I told God I would go into those deep waters but that I was scared. A steady peace came over me as He reminded me, "I am enough."

That was ten years ago. God and I had many more discussions since that day. Some were joyful, like the day six years ago when mom gave her life to the Lord! What a gift to be with her that day! We cried and rejoiced together. We have made great memories over the last ten years. Unfortunately, there were hurts too. Mom still battled addiction and all the ugliness that went with it. There were days when leaving mom's house, and I would get in my car, hurting and angry. I would pound the steering wheel, crying and telling God, "I don't want to do this anymore." He would lovingly wait while I let it all out, and always, His peace would come, and I would "hear," "I am enough." God never left Mom on that journey or me. He was always enough.

On May 24th, 2021, that journey came to an end. Mom's battle with addiction ended. She won the final battle. Because Mom said "Yes" to Him sex years ago, she is rejoicing in Heaven and thanking Him for his faithfulness and her deliverance. I thank God, He called me, that His Spirit moved me to say "Yes," that He was enough and that I will spend eternity with my mom, sober and free.

Karen Nabors

Epilogue

Whether you are a seeker, a new believer, or a seasoned follower, I trust you have found this book compelling and transforming. These God-stories, written by people just like you, from all walks of life, testify that God is working miracles in our lives today the same as in bible times.

I pray that you will experience a deeper relationship with God and follow His voice into His Kingdom.

Give this book to everyone you care about. Believe me, they will never be the same after reading this. What a gift!

Made in the USA
Columbia, SC
01 November 2021